curious about

WHALE SHARKS

BY MONIKA DAVIES

AMICUS LEARNING

What are you

curious about?

Curious About is published by
Amicus Learning, an imprint of Amicus
P.O. Box 227, Mankato, MN 56002
www.amicuspublishing.us

Editor: Ana Brauer
Series Designer: Kathleen Petelinsek
Book Designer and Photo Researcher: Sara Hood

Library of Congress Cataloging-in-Publication Data
Names: Davies, Monika, author.
Title: Curious about whale sharks / by Monika Davies.
Description: Mankato, MN : Amicus Learning, [2026] | Series: Curious about sharks | Includes bibliographical references and index. | Audience: Ages 6–9 | Audience: Grades 2–3 | Summary: "Are whale sharks peaceful? Can I swim with one? Learn about one of the ocean's gentle giants in this question-and-answer book for elementary-aged readers. Includes infographics, table of contents, glossary, books and websites for further research, and index"— Provided by publisher.
Identifiers: LCCN 2024048298 (print) | LCCN 2024048299 (ebook) | ISBN 9798892005081 (library binding) | ISBN 9798892005623 (paperback) | ISBN 9798892006163 (ebook)
Subjects: LCSH: Whale shark. | Whale shark—Ecology. | Whale shark—Conservation.
Classification: LCC QL638.95.R4 D39 2026 (print) | LCC QL638.95.R4 (ebook) | DDC 597.3—dc23/eng/20241207
LC record available at https://lccn.loc.gov/2024048298
LC ebook record available at https://lccn.loc.gov/2024048299

Photo Credits: Alamy Stock Photo/CMG, 17, Duncan Murrell, 2, 9, LOOK-foto, 2, 10–11, paul kennedy, 8, Pete Oxford, 4–5, Reinhard Dirscherl, cover, 1, SeaTops, 6-7; Dreamstime/Martin Helgemeir, 16; Getty Images/by wildestanimal, 3, 18–19, Johner Images, 12, Mathieu Meur/Stocktrek Images, 21, Samuel J Coe, 14–15, torstenvelden, 13; The Noun Project/Amethyst Studio, 22, 23, visual language, 22, zuri, 23; Vecteezy/om1947, 7

Printed in India

CHAPTER ONE 1

Is it a whale or a shark?

Whale sharks are known for being friendly.

It is a shark! Whales are mammals, but sharks are fish. Whale sharks are the world's largest fish. Their "whale-like" size gives them their name. They can grow up to 59 feet (18 meters) long. That's about as long as a bowling lane!

Can I swim with one?

Yes! Whale sharks are huge but harmless. Humans often swim beside these gentle giants. Whale sharks live in warm waters. They are found across the world. You might spot them in the western Atlantic Ocean.

Whale Shark Range Map

Each shark has a special pattern on their skin.

What is on their skin?

Spots and stripes create patterns on the dark gray skin of a whale shark. This pattern is one of a kind, like a fingerprint! This pattern can **identify** them. Scientists can track them by their patterns.

Remora fish will attach to whale sharks. They clean the shark and eat leftover scraps.

CHAPTER TWO

How do whale sharks eat?

Whale sharks cannot bite or chew their food. Instead, they are **filter** feeders. They open their wide mouth and gulp down ocean water. As the water flows down their throat, **tissue** with tiny holes catches their food. The remaining water leaves through the shark's **gills**.

Whale sharks usually hunt alone.

DID YOU KNOW?
A whale shark spends eight hours a day gulping about 10,000 gallons (37,854 liters) of ocean water to get enough food.

Whale sharks mostly eat **plankton.**

What do whale sharks eat?

Plankton is the top meal choice for whale sharks. Whale sharks also sometimes eat small fish, like sardines. They might eat up to 90 pounds (41 kg) of food every day. Some sharks travel far to satisfy their **appetite**!

Some plankton is too small to see. Whale sharks swim with their mouths open to catch the tiny animals.

How far do whale sharks travel?

Whale sharks travel long distances to find plankton.

It depends on the shark. Some whale sharks stick close to their home waters. But others will travel thousands of miles in a year. One whale shark traveled 12,000 miles (19,312 km) across the Pacific Ocean!

DID YOU KNOW?

Whale sharks move at slow speeds. They travel about 3 miles (4.8 km) per hour!

CHAPTER THREE

How are whale shark babies born?

Baby whale sharks sometimes swim alongside boats.

Whale shark babies come from **hatched** eggs inside their mother. Mothers give birth to live babies. Once born, whale sharks are on their own. They must take care of themselves without their mother's help.

Whale sharks are curious animals. They will often approach humans.

How long do whale sharks live?

A whale shark grows slowly. It takes 30 years to grow into an adult.

No one is quite sure. The oldest known whale shark was 50 years old. But some researchers think whale sharks might live to be over 100 years old. Others guess that number could be up to 150 years.

Are whale sharks endangered?

Yes. Whale sharks are the ocean's gentle giants. Their list of enemies is short. But their numbers are going down. Humans hunt them for food. Some sharks get caught in fishing nets. It is now against the law to catch a whale shark.

DID YOU KNOW?

Some scientists think only about 1 in 10 whale sharks make it to adulthood.

Many countries help
keep whale sharks safe.

STAY CURIOUS!

ASK MORE QUESTIONS

Where are whale sharks usually found?

What other sharks are filter feeders?

Try a BIG QUESTION:
How can humans take care of whale sharks?

SEARCH FOR ANSWERS

Search the library catalog or the Internet.
A librarian, teacher, or parent can help you.

Using Keywords
Find the looking glass.

Keywords are the most important words in your question.

If you want to know about:

- whale shark ranges, type: WHALE SHARK OCEANS
- which sharks are filter feeders, type: FILTER FEEDER SHARKS

LEARN MORE

FIND GOOD SOURCES

Some are better than others. An adult can help you look.
Here are some good, safe sources.

Books

Whale Shark
by Jenna Lee Gleisner, 2020.

Whale Sharks
by Rachel Grack, 2025.

Internet Sites

Britannica Kids: Whale Shark
https://kids.britannica.com/kids/article/whale-shark/602319
Britannica Kids is full of kid-friendly, fact-checked articles.

National Geographic Kids: Whale Shark
https://kids.nationalgeographic.com/animals/fish/facts/whale-sharks
National Geographic Kids is a great source to discover information about animals.

Every effort has been made to ensure that these websites are appropriate for children. However, because of the nature of the Internet, it is impossible to guarantee that these sites will remain active indefinitely or that their contents will not be altered.

SHARE AND TAKE ACTION

Whale sharks are endangered.
With an adult or your class, come up with ideas to protect the ocean animals.

Draw a picture of a whale shark. Include its unique spots and stripes.
Compare your picture with a friend's drawing.

Help take care of the oceans for whale sharks. Do not throw garbage in the ocean.
Join a beach clean-up to pick up litter.

GLOSSARY

appetite A physical desire for food.

filter Something that is used to catch something and remove it from a liquid as it passes through it.

gill An organ in fish used to get oxygen from water.

hatch To be born by coming out of an egg.

identify To show what something is.

plankton The very small animal and plant life in an ocean, lake, or river.

tissue The material that forms parts in an animal.

INDEX

About the Author

Monika Davies is a Canadian author of over 60 books for young readers. She thinks sharks are fascinating—and hopes you agree! When Monika isn't writing, you can find her strolling by the ocean, reading books too quickly, or trying to keep her seven plants alive.